Lesley A. DuTemple

Lerner Publications Company
Minneapolis

For Jim—my friend and spouse extraordinaire

A&E and **BIOGRAPHY** are trademarks of the A&E Television Networks, registered in the United States and other countries.

Some of the people profiled in this series have also been featured in A&E's acclaimed BIOGRAPHY series, which is available on videocassette from A&E Home Video. Call 1-800-423-1212 to order.

Lerner Publications Company
A division of Lerner Publishing Group
241 First Avenue North
Minneapolis, MN 55401 U.S.A.

Website address: www.lernerbooks.com

Library of Congress Cataloging-in-Publication Data

DuTemple, Lesley A.
    Jacques Cousteau/Lesley A. DuTemple.
        p.   c.m — (A&E biography)
    Includes bibliographical references and index.
    Summary: Examines the life and accomplishments of the
oceanographer Jacques Cousteau, describing his work studying and
filming the undersea world.
    ISBN 0-8225-4979-4 (lib. bdg. : alk. paper)
    1. Cousteau, Jacques Yves—Juvenile literature. 2. Oceanographers—
France—Biography—Juvenile literature. [1. Cousteau, Jacques Yves. 2.
Oceanographers.] I. Title. II. Series.
GC30.C68 D88 2000
551.46'0092—dc21
    [B]   99-038342

Manufactured in the United States of America
2 3 4 5 6 7 – JR – 06 05 04 03 02 01

CONTENTS

Jacques Cousteau's fascination with the undersea world grew stronger after a visit to the popular beach area of La Mourillon in southern France.

Chapter **ONE**

DISCOVERY

ONE WARM SUMMER MORNING IN **1936,** JACQUES-Yves Cousteau waded into the clear water of the Mediterranean Sea. The twenty-six-year-old French naval officer was off duty from his post at a nearby base in the town of Toulon, France. A short trolley ride took him to any number of beaches, including this one, at the beach area of La Mourillon, where he swam nearly every day. On this particular morning, the tall, skinny Frenchman was trying an experiment. He was wearing goggles.

Few swimmers at that time wore goggles. But several years earlier, while on duty in the South Seas, an area of the southern Pacific Ocean, Jacques had been surprised to see some pearl divers wearing funny-looking goggles. He had never seen anything like that and wondered what purpose the goggles served.

Back in France, he'd decided to try goggles himself. He had brainstormed with a couple of friends, and they had decided that aviator goggles—the kind worn by pilots—would have to do. Jacques wanted to know if goggles would keep saltwater out of a swimmer's eyes. The sting of saltwater—the "salty obstacle," as he called it—was a constant source of irritation to him.

Plunging into the shallow water near shore, Jacques caught his breath in astonishment. The goggles did indeed keep the water out of his eyes. But what amazed him even more was that he could see everything so well. What had previously looked like a blur, viewed through burning eyes, now appeared in sharp focus. Lit by shafts of sunlight shimmering down through the water was a vivid world of color and movement.

"I was astounded by what I saw," Jacques wrote later. "Rocks were covered with green, brown, and silver forests of algae." Brilliant fishes darted about. Running out of breath, he stood up. "I saw a trolley car, people, electric-light poles." Plunging back underwater, "I was in a jungle never seen by those who floated on the opaque roof," he wrote.

That day, Jacques-Yves Cousteau's life began, as he later said, to "run headlong down an immutable course." He swore he would "design, build, and operate devices that would deliver me to the sunken ridges of the silent world." That passion led him to invent many innovative machines, including the equipment we now call scuba (which stands for self-contained underwater breathing apparatus). Jacques's scuba invention was so successful that at the time of his death in 1997 there were more than 10 million divers in the United States alone.

Jacques also went on to guide millions of people below the "opaque roof" of the water by filming the underwater world, developing many pioneering techniques in the process. He wrote best-selling books, produced television documentaries, and made movies that won Academy Awards. As he grew older, he became an ardent conservationist, protesting pollution and other human actions that damage the ocean.

Throughout Jacques-Yves Cousteau's life, the ocean was a constant. His abiding respect for it determined, in many ways, the course of his life. "Sometimes we are lucky enough to know that our lives have been changed, to discard the old, embrace the new," he later wrote. "It happened to me at La Mourillon on that summer's day, when my eyes were opened on the sea."

One-year-old Jacques is shown here with his brother Pierre-
Antoine, age five.

Chapter **TWO**

BEGINNINGS

JACQUES-YVES COUSTEAU WAS BORN ON JUNE 11, 1910, in Saint-André-de-Cubzac, a quiet town in the Bordeaux region of France. His parents, Elizabeth and Daniel Cousteau, were both natives of Saint-André-de-Cubzac. The couple lived in the bustling city of Paris, where Daniel worked for an American millionaire, James Hazen Hyde, as Hyde's private secretary.

The Cousteaus loved the glamour of Paris, but they also had strong ties to the town of their birth. Just before Jacques was born, Elizabeth returned to Saint-André-de-Cubzac with Jacques's older brother, four-year-old Pierre-Antoine, to be with her family and friends during the birth. Jacques-Yves came into the world surrounded by loving relatives.

When Jacques was a few weeks old, Elizabeth took him and Pierre-Antoine back to Paris by train. The trip set the tone for much of Jacques's early childhood. James Hyde traveled extensively and expected Daniel Cousteau to accompany him. Where Daniel went, the rest of the Cousteau family followed. Jacques quickly learned to adjust to constant travel and ever-changing surroundings. One of his earliest memories was of being rocked to sleep on a train.

When Jacques was four, his parents took their boys to a fashionable seaside resort at Deauville. Jacques was mesmerized by the sparkling Mediterranean. He quickly learned to swim, an unusual achievement at that time for a child so young.

But Jacques was rarely allowed to swim. For he was a sickly boy and swimming was too rigorous for him. Small and skinny and anemic, he seemed to catch every illness that came along. His parents took him to doctor after doctor, to no avail.

When Jacques was about seven, his father went to work for another American millionaire, Eugene Higgins. Higgins also loved to travel, indulging his passion for golf, fishing, horses, and fast boats. He, too, required that Daniel travel with him.

For a while, Elizabeth continued to accompany Daniel. But more and more, she stayed home, fretting over their second son. She and Daniel thought the many trips might be exposing Jacques to new illnesses, or the schedule might be too hard on him.

When the Cousteau boys were old enough, their parents enrolled them in a French boarding school. Jacques would not have to keep up with Eugene Higgins's schedule anymore. Although Elizabeth disliked leaving her children behind, she hoped school life would improve Jacques's health. Jacques was not a great student, but he passed his courses. His health, however, continued to be frail.

Then Eugene Higgins stepped in. Exercise was the best way for Jacques to gain strength, Higgins said. He advised Elizabeth and Daniel to let eight-year-old Jacques swim.

Being told to swim for his health was a dream come true for Jacques. He loved it. He swam in the ocean, he swam in lakes, he swam in any pool he could find. He was often cold, but, over time, swimming did make him stronger.

In addition to accompanying Eugene Higgins around Europe, the Cousteaus also accompanied him to the United States. In 1920, while the couple was staying in New York, they brought their sons to the United States and sent them to a summer camp at Harvey's Lake in Vermont.

Clean-up was a part of camp life anywhere, but at Harvey's Lake, counselors gave new meaning to the term. "Clean-up" meant tidying everything, even the bottom of the lake. Every day campers dove along the shore, removing debris from the water.

The daily dives became ten-year-old Jacques's

favorite activity. He tried to stay underwater as long as he could. One day, he tried breathing through a pipe that extended above the water's surface. He found he couldn't. A dive could last only as long as a boy could hold his breath.

Water wasn't Jacques's only passion. He was even more fascinated by machines—how they worked and what they could do. At the age of eleven, he constructed a model of a marine crane almost as tall as he was. Another time, he built a battery-operated car. No piece of machinery was safe in the Cousteau house. Jacques took everything apart. Luckily, he was equally quick to put things back together.

One machine that particularly interested Jacques was a relatively new invention, the movie camera. At thirteen he saved up his allowance and bought one. Of course, the first thing Jacques did was take the camera apart to see how it worked, then put it back together again. After that, Jacques shot roll after roll of home movies.

Meanwhile, Jacques's interest in schoolwork declined. Bored, he earned a reputation at the high school he was attending as a poor student. Machines were his only interest, he claimed. Machines did such magical things! He wanted to drop all his other subjects and study only machines.

When teachers refused to indulge him, he began causing trouble. He cut classes, broke things, and lied about his misdeeds. His "boredom" reached a new high the day he broke seventeen windows. Jacques could explain: he wanted the windows to look as though they'd been shot out by rampaging cowboys.

No one was amused. Jacques's teachers had had enough, and he was expelled. His parents, dismayed by their son's behavior, packed him off to one of the strictest boarding schools in France.

Jacques, front, second from left, *mugged for a family photo in 1915 in his home village of Saint-André-de-Cubzac.*

LONGING FOR ADVENTURE

At sixteen, Jacques found himself in Ribeauvillé, France, at a school so strict it resembled a military boarding school. Misbehavior was not tolerated. Discipline and hard work were demanded of each student.

Surprisingly, Jacques responded to the demands of his new school with a burst of enthusiasm. Maybe he had no time to be bored, maybe he matured, or maybe he just decided to buckle down. Whatever the reason, Jacques often studied well into the night. He pulled his grades up and even began to excel. Delighting everyone, including himself, he graduated with honors in 1929 at the age of nineteen.

That achievement didn't mean, however, that Jacques wanted more formal education. He didn't. What Jacques wanted more than anything was adventure. He wanted to travel the world.

One of the best ways to see the world was to join the navy, which is exactly what Jacques did. In 1930, he passed the highly competitive entrance exam for the prestigious French naval academy at Brest. Jacques studied for two years at the academy.

For his third year of training, Jacques was sent on a cruise that would take him around the world. He took his beloved movie camera along, shooting roll after roll of film, including footage of his encounter with the pearl divers in the South Seas.

The training cruise ended, and Jacques found himself back in France. He edited his film into a full-length newsreel and showed it to his friends and family. Then he was off again, this time to the Far East, where he spent 1933 to 1935 aboard a French naval cruiser as well as ashore in Shanghai.

Upon returning from the Far East, Jacques looked for a way to continue his adventurous lifestyle. It would be exciting to fly. The French navy had its own aviation course, and its pilots seemed to have the most adventuresome options in the navy. Jacques decided to become a navy flier and enrolled in the year-long course. He did all the required work with ease.

One evening in early 1936, Jacques borrowed his father's luxury sports car, a snappy little Salmson, to attend the wedding of a friend in the Vosges Mountains. The Salmson was small and fast, and Jacques loved to drive it. As he sped along in the dark over the road's sharp curves, the car's headlights suddenly went out. Slamming on the brakes, he spun out of control and crashed head-on into a retaining wall.

Jacques remembered the accident vividly—remembered lying alone, bleeding, thinking he was going to die. He looked up at the sky and the stars. "My God," he thought to himself, "how lucky I was to have seen so many things in my life."

FIGHTING BACK

Jacques was rushed to a hospital. For days he hovered in and out of consciousness. When he finally came to, he learned that his left arm had been broken in five places. Worse, his right arm, which was also broken, was paralyzed and badly infected. His doctor told him that it needed to be amputated.

Dizzy and sick with fever, Jacques wouldn't hear of it. His doctor reluctantly agreed not to amputate. Jacques's parents visited him a few days later and found him thin, weak, and racked with pain. But he was determined to regain the use of his arms.

Physical therapy was slow and painful. The damage to the bones and muscles of Jacques's right arm had been extensive. After months of difficult work, Jacques did regain the use of both of his arms. His right arm remained slightly twisted, however, for the rest of his life.

By the end of 1936, Jacques was ready to resume active duty. But even taking the most optimistic view, Jacques knew the navy would never let him fly. Instead, Lieutenant Jacques-Yves Cousteau was assigned to the navy's base at Toulon as an artillery instructor.

Cousteau's World

NORTH ATLANTIC OCEAN

SOUTH ATLANTIC OCEAN

EUROPE

ENGLAND
London
Deauville
Marne R.
Brest
Paris
FRANCE
La Rochelle
Saint-André-de-Cubzac
Tagus R.
Lisbon
PORTUGAL
Ribeauvillé
VOSGES MTNS.
Vichy
Area of inset
MALTA
MEDITERRANEAN SEA

AFRICA

EGYPT
Gulf of Suez
Port Sudan
Nile R.
SUDAN
RED SEA
SAUDI ARABIA
Persian Gulf

ASIA

CHINA
Shanghai
SOUTH CHINA SEA
Singapore

INDIAN OCEAN

SEYCHELLES
Assumption Island

Inset — FRANCE

MONACO
Antibes
Cannes
Marseille
Toulon
Sorgue
Avignon
Grand Congloué Island
Sanary
Porquerolles Island
MEDITERRANEAN SEA
FRANCE

Early diving equipment was heavy and cumbersome. A helmet limits this diver's view, and a hose to supply air connects him to his ship.

Chapter **THREE**

EARLY INVENTIONS

AT THE BASE IN TOULON, JACQUES MADE FRIENDS with fellow lieutenant Philippe Taillez, who urged Jacques to swim as therapy for his twisted arm. Jacques could no longer swim as smoothly or as fast as he had before his accident, but daily swims did help his right arm grow stronger and straighter.

As Jacques swam and dove, he couldn't help remembering the South Seas pearl divers he had filmed on his voyage around the world. Even as he wondered about the goggles they wore, he asked another question: how did they stay underwater so long?

Divers had long wanted a way to breathe underwater. Since the 1800s, divers had used equipment that tried to solve this problem. They wore diving suits

and helmets with air piped to them from an air supply on the surface. But the suits and helmets were so
heavy and cumbersome that divers could barely move.
They could only plod slowly along the water's bottom,
going no farther than their air hoses allowed.

While stationed in Toulon, Jacques also met Frédéric
Dumas. Didi, as Frédéric was called, lived in Sanary, a
beautiful little beach town about seven miles from
Toulon. Didi spent most of his time on the water.
When Didi wasn't on his boat, he was camping on the
beach or swimming. Jacques and Philippe began
spending every free moment with Didi.

The threesome spent many hours swimming and diving along the shore near Sanary. A favorite sport was
plunging into the water from large rocks that dotted
the shoreline. The three men were soon diving to
depths of 30 feet.

WORKING TOGETHER

It was Didi and Philippe who had brainstormed with
Jacques to come up with the idea of the aviator goggles. As well as the goggles worked, Jacques was determined to make them better. He began designing
variations of them, looking for a way to adapt them
for underwater use.

Jacques also made snorkels out of garden hoses. And
he experimented with ways to control buoyancy—the
tendency of a human body to float. Pushing down off
rocks helped a person dive more deeply than he or

The diving trio of Jacques, Philippe, and Didi spent most of their free time diving near Sanary, France, above. *Here they tested their inventions (goggles, snorkels, and weight belts), seeking ways to dive ever deeper into the sea.*

she otherwise could. But to go deeper, more weight was needed. Jacques tried making different kinds of weight belts that would help a person sink, yet still allow him or her to return to the surface.

With each design, Jacques got Philippe and Didi to help him test the new item. Each of the men eagerly reported his own results to the others. All three agreed that Jacques's goggles and weight belts worked well.

Jacques's snorkels, however, were a dismal failure. Once a diver descended more than a few feet, he couldn't get any air, no matter how hard he sucked on the garden hose. Rather than becoming discouraged, Jacques grew increasingly fascinated with the prospect of staying underwater longer and exploring the ocean's hidden worlds.

At about that time, while on a trip to Paris, Jacques met a lovely young woman, Simone Melchoir. She came from a seafaring family. In fact, most of the men in her family had been admirals in the navy. The biggest regret in the eighteen years of her life was that she couldn't choose a career at sea. That path was closed to her because she was female.

Simone was the perfect companion for Jacques. A beautiful girl with soft blond hair, she was also funny and vivacious and as much in love with the sea as Jacques was. The two became inseparable. They spent hours talking as they roamed the tree-lined streets of Paris. When Simone traveled to Toulon to see Jacques, they spent their time at the beach, wandering along the shore or swimming in the turquoise water.

The two made plans for the future. Simone's parents decided that Jacques's career looked promising, so they gave their blessing to the pair. On July 12, 1937, Jacques and Simone were married. The newlyweds established their first home in Sanary.

Simone dove often with Jacques and his friends. In no time at all, she became an accomplished diver. She continued to dive even after she became pregnant. By the middle of the pregnancy, though, she watched from the beach.

Simone and Jacques Cousteau married in 1937. Simone shared Jacques's love for diving and became an expert diver herself.

By this time, Jacques could make impressive dives. With nothing more than a lungful of air, he could descend to depths of 50 to 60 feet. Even so, he coveted an underwater source of air. "We wanted breathing equipment, not so much to go deeper," he later explained, "but to stay longer." In order "simply to live a while in the new world," as Jacques wished, a diver ought to be able to breathe and move about as freely as any underwater creature.

Perhaps one key to an efficient underwater breathing system was the gas a diver breathed. The air people normally breathe contains only 21 percent oxygen. The rest is 78 percent nitrogen and 1 percent other gases. People at the time had experimented with oxygen and found that it becomes toxic at great depth (although the exact depth was not known). Jacques and his friends knew of the problems with oxygen, but they also knew how little the problems were really understood. The unknown always had a seductive power over Jacques. His lifelong motto was *Il faut aller voir* (We must go see for ourselves).

Setting out for themselves to see what would happen, the trio created a breathing system with a gas mask, an inner tube, and a bottle of oxygen. Jacques was elected to try it out. Less than one minute into his dive, he suffered a seizure. He kept control long enough to jettison his weight belt and then lost consciousness. Nearly lifeless, he floated to the surface, where his friends hauled his body out of the water.

Jacques recovered. Although concerned with safety, he always wanted to push on. "In testing devices in which one's life is at stake," he said, "such accidents induce zeal for improvement." He began tinkering again with the breathing system, sure that the device—not the oxygen itself—had somehow caused his seizure. Then he dove again, this time to a depth of 45 feet. Again, he convulsed. And again, he was rescued. Later, he said he could not even remember having jettisoned his weight belt. "I came very near drowning," he wrote. "It was the end of my interest in oxygen."

Rather than giving up, the trio turned to a new idea.

They would use compressed air. The technology for pumping a large quantity of normal air into a small tank had been developed. Divers weren't benefiting from it, however. One problem was that compressed air is under great pressure, so when released from a tank, it escapes in one big "whoosh."

Jacques decided to consult with Simone's father, Henri Melchoir, who had retired from the navy. Henri Melchoir had become an executive with Air Liquide— a French company that manufactured, sold, and transported gases such as nitrogen, oxygen, and carbon dioxide. He was familiar with the most advanced uses of compressed air. Henri Melchoir acknowledged that it would be possible to design a breathing system using compressed air. What was missing, the two men agreed, was a valve to control the flow of the air. And because Jacques wanted divers to be able to breathe without having to turn a valve on and off, the valve needed to be self-regulating.

Shortly afterward, in 1938, Simone gave birth to a little boy. She and Jacques named him Jean-Michel. Jacques's happiness was complete. He had an adventurous wife who liked to dive, he was a father, and he was successfully focusing his search for a way to breathe underwater. Jacques was convinced that, in no time at all, he would be a "manfish."

Even though Germany bombed Toulon during World War II, nearby Sanary remained untouched. Cousteau worked for a time at the navy base in Toulon but lived in Sanary with his growing family.

Chapter **FOUR**

WARTIME WORK

IN **1938, G**ERMANY, **LED BY A**DOLF **H**ITLER, invaded Austria, beginning the chain of catastrophic events that would come to be known as World War II. For the time being, however, little changed in France. Jacques continued to work at the base in Toulon and to return to Simone and baby Jean-Michel every evening.

In September 1939, France and Great Britain declared war on Germany. Jacques became a gunnery officer on a French naval cruiser, the *Dupleix*. The crew drilled frequently, but they remained in the port at Toulon. Although France opposed Hitler, it was not ready to send its navy to fight him.

Soon after war was declared, several torpedo boats

from the British navy, also stationed in Toulon, needed to depart. But a heavy steel cable had gotten tangled around the shaft and propeller blades of one of the boats. Jacques volunteered to dive under the boat to survey the situation. After taking a look, he believed the boat could be freed from the snarl, but he needed help.

Jacques selected five other divers from his ship. Together they dove and hacked away at the steel cable. After diving repeatedly for several hours, surfacing for air with each dive, they finally freed the propeller.

Back on their own ship, the divers were hailed as the torpedo boat sailed past. As Jacques wrote, "The crew turned out in a line at the rail and gave three cheers for the crazy Frenchmen."

But the work had taken its toll. The divers were so exhausted they could barely stand. "That day I learned that heavy exertion underwater was madness," Jacques later wrote. "It was absolutely necessary to have breathing apparatus to do such jobs."

Then Hitler rolled into Poland. France still did nothing. The French people dubbed the war *"drôle de guerre"* (the phony war).

On June 4, 1940, Germany bombed the outskirts of Paris. On June 10, Italy joined Germany by declaring war on France and by immediately sending squadrons to bomb Toulon. Damage to the base was light, and Sanary, where Simone and Jean-Michel were living, wasn't hit at all. Even so, three days later, the entire

French fleet at Toulon was ordered out of port. Clustered together in the harbor, the ships would be easy targets in the event of more bombing raids. They would be safer on the open sea.

The next day—June 14, 1940—Hitler's army took control of Paris. The French government surrendered. Under the terms of the surrender, the French would still rule the lower portion of France. That government, established in Vichy, would be headed by Marshal Henri Philippe Pétain. It soon became clear, however, that Pétain was a puppet who took orders from Hitler. In truth, all of France was occupied by Germany. Most French people were outraged.

All this was confusing enough, but to make matters worse, when Germany claimed France, Britain contacted the original French government and demanded that command of the French navy be turned over to Britain. Britain had withstood relentless bombing attacks by the German air force. It could not withstand a naval attack as well, particularly if the large, well-equipped French navy fell into Hitler's hands.

The British demand threw the French navy into chaos. The crews of some French ships turned themselves over to the British. Other crews, including that of the *Dupleix,* were uncertain about what to do and began turning back toward Toulon. Britain countered with a threat that it would bomb any French warships returning to port.

The *Dupleix* now faced attack by one of its allies.

But the ship returned to Toulon without incident. To the dismay of patriotic Frenchmen, Pétain's government stepped in and ordered all the returned ships to stay put.

Despite the seemingly explosive situation, nothing happened. Jacques was assigned to guard duty at a nearby fort. Simone and Jean-Michel still lived in Sanary, along with a new baby, Philippe (named after the Cousteaus' friend Philippe Taillez). By the end of 1940, there was little military action in the Mediterranean and little for Jacques to do at the fort. He kept short hours and spent time with Simone, Jean-Michel, and the new baby.

Jacques's life only appeared to be quiet, however. Secretly, he had joined an underground movement of French people working against the German occupation. Led from a distance by General Charles de Gaulle, who had fled to London, the people in the French Resistance fought Hitler bitterly, however they could. Jacques helped in several ways. Once, he and a group under his command dove under the ships of the French fleet, placing enough explosives to sink every ship. The fleet could be destroyed if necessary to prevent Hitler from using the ships.

Another time, Jacques impersonated an Italian officer and spent four tense hours in an Italian military office, furtively photographing top secret documents— including the Italian naval signals code. Together with Philippe, Jacques also did underwater spying. By approaching underwater, they could enter German shoreline operations without being seen. They reported all information they gathered to leaders in the French Resistance.

DIVING EXPERIMENTS

In 1942, Jacques was transferred to French Naval Intelligence in Marseilles, another port city on the Mediterranean. Jacques was convinced that an underwater breathing system could help the war effort. Such a system would help divers in laying mines, disarming mines, and spying. Jacques's new commander agreed and assigned Jacques to continue his experiments as much as his other work permitted.

One experimental project was testing some new equipment known as the Fernez diving apparatus, or the Fernez pump. Jacques wasn't too pleased with the equipment. "It tethered a man to the surface and unnecessarily wasted half the air," he later wrote, and thus was no improvement over the cumbersome diving suits already in use. The tether was a pipe that carried air, pumped from a tank on the surface, to a diver underwater. One day, while breathing with the Fernez pump from 40 feet underwater, Jacques felt all the air shut off. He held his breath and shot to the surface. The pipe had broken, and he was fortunate not to have drowned.

During the Cousteau family's time in Marseilles, German bombers bombed the naval base at Toulon.

THE EVOLUTION OF DIVING GEAR

ollowing is a timeline of early underwater explorers and their diving inventions.
- **1690** Edmund Halley (who also discovered and named a comet) patented the first diving bell. Capable of holding several men, this device had barrels of air attached to it and could submerge to 60 feet for ninety minutes.
- **1837** Augustus Siebe invented a watertight, air-containing rubber suit with a large helmet attached. The suit was connected to an air pump on the surface that supplied air to the diver.
- **1876** Henry Fleuss developed a self-contained diving apparatus that used compressed oxygen rather than compressed air. Although it turned out that pure oxygen was toxic below approximately 25 feet, the apparatus did allow divers to submerge for up to three hours.
- **1910** John Haldane published a paper titled "The Prevention of Compressed-Air Illness."

Edmund Halley's diving bell could contain several men underwater for ninety minutes.

By showing that deep-water divers need to return to the surface in careful stages, Haldane laid the groundwork for staged decompression charts.

- **1920s** The United States researched the safety of a mix of helium and oxygen for deep dives.
- **1930** William Beebe descended 1,426 feet in a small round bathyscaphe of his own making.
- **1930s** Guy Gilpatric pioneered the use of rubber flight goggles with glass lenses for skin diving. In 1938, he published *The Compleat Goggler,* a book on amateur diving. Jacques-Yves Cousteau was one of the book's first readers.
- **1933** Yves Le Prieur invented a breathing apparatus that combined a specially designed valve with a high-pressure air tank. However, the diver had to open a tap in order to receive air. Exhaled air escaped under the diver's mask. Jacques Cousteau dove with this apparatus in the late 1930s but noted that "the continuous discharge of air allowed only short submersions."

- **1942–1943** Jacques-Yves Cousteau and Émile Gagnan redesigned a car regulator to automatically provide air to a diver with the slightest intake of breath. They patented their device as the "aqualung."

William Beebe made a descent in his own bathyscaphe in 1930.

This ensured that Hitler's army could move in to capture the fleet. Jacques and Simone, asleep in Marseilles, were awakened by the sound of planes overhead. Quickly turning the radio on, they learned the news. The French ships that Jacques had booby-trapped had blown up in a roar of explosions and flame. "The announcer's voice broke as he read the roll of ships, which included the . . . *Dupleix*," Jacques remembered. "Simone and I wept by the radio."

During the German occupation, German soldiers patrolled the beaches and sometimes prevented swimmers from entering the water. This could have had a devastating effect on Jacques's diving. But the patrols rarely interfered with Jacques. He had an *ordre de mission*, a permit from the International Committee for the Exploration of the Mediterranean. Whenever Jacques presented his *ordre*, even the toughest German soldiers let him through.

Later, Jacques learned that the German government had been spending millions to develop military underwater equipment. Some of the German teams working on the project may have been diving in the same locations as Jacques. Luckily, none of the German beach patrols ever asked Jacques exactly what he and his team were doing.

A Long-Awaited Breakthrough
In December 1942, Jacques's father-in-law arranged for Jacques to meet Émile Gagnan, an engineer at Air

Liquide in Paris. An expert on industrial gas equipment, Gagnan nodded encouragingly as Jacques explained his latest ideas about an underwater breathing system, then interrupted to say, "Something like this?" Gagnan handed Jacques a small valve Gagnan had developed to enable cars to run on cooking fuel. The valve was necessary because, during the war, civilians found it difficult to purchase gas. As Gagnan pointed out to Jacques, "The problem is somewhat the same as yours."

Jacques was delighted. Gagnan's device was self-regulating! Jacques and Gagnan began to adapt it, and Jacques realized he had found someone who loved machines as much as he did. Within weeks, the pair had their first automatic air regulator ready to test.

For the test dive, the two inventors selected a lonely stretch of the Marne River nearby. Jacques waded in while Gagnan stood on the bank, watching anxiously.

As soon as Jacques began to breathe with the regulator, he could tell it didn't work. He got a good supply of air when he was horizontal, but when he moved into any other position, the air supply shut off.

Disappointed, the two men headed back to Paris. They analyzed the problem all the way back. Before they had arrived, they knew they had a solution. Within weeks they had modified their design and tested it in a tank of water, where it worked perfectly. They applied for a patent and gave their device a name. They had invented the "aqualung."

With the invention of the aqualung, divers could remain underwater for longer periods of time—and film what they saw.

Chapter **FIVE**

FILMING WITH THE AQUALUNG

ONE MORNING IN JUNE 1943, AFTER RETURNING to Toulon, Jacques went to the railway station and picked up a large wooden case that had been shipped to him from Paris. Inside was an assembly of three metal cylinders about as big as a large backpack and an automatic air regulator the size of an alarm clock. Gagnan had shipped him the aqualung.

Not long after, Jacques, Didi, and Philippe got their first chance to dive with the aqualung. Remembering that the earlier breathing apparatus had worked only when he was horizontal, Jacques did loops, somersaults, and barrel rolls. "I stood upside down on one finger and burst out laughing . . . ," he wrote. "Nothing I did altered the automatic rhythm of air."

He could breathe! And he could move as freely as he wished. The aqualung weighed more than fifty pounds, but once in the water, it became manageably light. So did a man's body. "Delivered from gravity . . . I flew around in space," Jacques wrote. The aqualung was everything Jacques had hoped for.

That summer the Cousteaus rented a villa in Sanary, and Didi, Philippe and his family, and another couple lived with them. The group was one big, happy family.

With the aqualung, Jacques and his friends had all the underwater freedom that they'd hoped for. They made hundreds of dives, descending deeper and deeper. As their depth increased, they left the sun behind them. Here was what Jacques called a "twilight world." While sea life in 10 feet of water glowed with color, at 100 feet, everything was murky and dim.

In experimenting with the limits of the aqualung, Jacques and his companions were also exploring the limits of the human body. No one had ever dived so deep before or stayed underwater so long with a self-contained breathing apparatus. No one really knew what effects long-term, deepwater submersion might have on the human body. With the aqualung, Jacques could blaze new trails in underwater science.

SHIPWRECKS

Jacques, Didi, and Philippe had often regaled their friends with tales of undersea glories. Deepsea diving was too dangerous a sport for most people, though.

Besides, aqualungs were not commercially available. Jacques decided that, since he couldn't take his friends into the underwater world, he would bring it to them. He found an obsolete Kinamo movie camera and bought it for twenty-five dollars.

Although Jacques had come up with the aqualung and with many of the diving plans for himself and Philippe and Didi, the threesome had always worked

Equipped with aqualungs, Jacques and his fellow divers could satisfy their desire to explore the beauty under the sea. With the machines on their backs, divers viewed a world filled with formerly undiscovered fish, animals, and plants.

as a team. Filming was no different. They worked together to figure out the best way to film underwater.
They built a watertight case to house the camera and
then had a fine lens ground. The next step was find-
ing 35mm movie film. During wartime, there was
none to be had. Jacques bought several fifty-foot rolls
of regular film and spliced the negatives together in
the darkroom to make movie film.

Jacques took his patched-together film and plunged
beneath the waves. His first underwater film was
titled *Eighteen Meters Down*. Although primitive by
modern standards, the film gave Jacques's friends
their first view of life beneath the waves. A few years
later, when Jacques showed the film at the newly or-
ganized Cannes Film Festival, an amazed public got
its first look at the wonders of the undersea world.

For the next film, the choice of subject matter was
unanimous among the trio. They would film the
sunken ships of the French fleet. Since the night two
years earlier, when the ships had been destroyed, the
wrecks had preyed on the minds of the divers. Didi in
particular was obsessed with the idea of exploring
them. In the summer of 1943, equipped with a new
aqualung and movie camera, the threesome began to
film the ships.

To get an idea of what they might be up against,
Jacques, Philippe, and Didi first filmed the wreck of
an old British steamer, the *Dalton*, which was easier
to reach than most of the sunken French fleet. Sunk

on Christmas night 1928, the *Dalton* lay 50 feet underwater. After fifteen years in the sea, the ship was festooned with seaweed, colorful algae, and mussels.

On film and off, the three men explored the *Dalton* and the other wrecks. Underwater, even ordinary objects were worthy of exploration—and humor. Jacques told of an incident on the wreck *Tozeur*. "Under the bridge we found the captain's bathroom. Didi swam down and lay in the bathtub. It was quite lifelike—a near-naked man in a bathtub. I almost lost my mouthpiece laughing."

Jacques made two films of shipwreck explorations: *Danger under the Sea* in 1943 and *Landscapes of Silence* in 1944. The films showed the divers cavorting through the sunken shipwrecks, swimming in and out of hatches, and playing with fish. A few years later, both were shown at the Cannes Film Festival. They astonished their audiences.

BLOOD THE COLOR OF EMERALDS

As underwater filmmakers, Jacques, Didi, and Philippe were solving problems no land photographer had ever faced. Cameras had to be housed in watertight boxes, which made it impossible to adjust them the way a land photographer would. One invention of Jacques's was a clothespin lever to adjust the lens of a camera inside a box.

Underwater lighting was something that really intrigued them. For many years, divers had assumed that sea life in deeper water lacked the vibrant color of sea life in shallower water. Then one day, Jacques and Didi were spearfishing 120 feet below the surface. When Didi speared a large grouper fish, a thick cloud of blood stained the water. "It was the color of emeralds . . . ," Jacques remembered. "Dumas and I looked at each other wildly." Didi led the way to the surface. "At fifty-five feet the blood turned dark brown," Jacques wrote. "At twenty feet it was pink. On the surface it flowed red."

The two soon descended to 160 feet, taking a studio light powered by their ship's generator. In the darkness, Didi snapped the light on. "What an explosion!" Jacques wrote. "The beam exposed a dazzling harlequinade of color." Here were "sensational reds and oranges as opulent as a Matisse" painting. They had discovered that deepwater life glows with every color of the rainbow. The distorting quality of water and the low levels of light at great depths had kept them from being able to see the colors before. As Jacques expressed it, "The living hues of the twilight world appeared for the first time since the creation of the world."

Meanwhile, the threesome also kept thinking about the military applications of the aqualung. Before they had built the aqualung, they had dreamed of various wartime uses for such a device. Now they knew exactly what they could do with it: they wanted to establish an underwater commando unit. In November

1944, Jacques journeyed to London to propose that the British use the aqualung in such units. Although the British were interested, they dismissed Jacques's proposal as coming too late in the war.

By the end of 1944, France was liberated from German control, and the French navy assigned its officers to peacetime roles. Jacques was transferred to a desk job and Philippe was assigned to the position of forest ranger. Only Didi, a civilian, was free to remain at the beach. For the moment, diving and filming would have to wait.

Jacques recruited talented and eager divers to help him explore
sunken ships and live mines as well as living sea creatures.

Chapter SIX

THE UNDERSEA RESEARCH GROUP

JACQUES KNEW A DESK JOB WAS NOT FOR HIM. Besides, the way he saw it, anyone could do his assignment. Likewise, Philippe was at a loss as a forest ranger. The problem was to convince the French navy that they were more useful underwater.

Just a few days into his new job, Jacques took matters into his own hands. "There were hundreds of jobs for divers in the scuttled fleet and in ships torpedoed at sea," as Jacques reasoned. He traveled to Paris and met with officers of the French navy. He showed them one of the films of Didi and Philippe finning through shipwrecks. "The next day," he wrote, "I was on my way to Toulon with a commission to resume diving experiments."

Jacques was authorized to form a formal unit in the French navy, the Undersea Research Group. Within days, Jacques, Philippe, and Didi were together again. Because Philippe was the senior officer, he was named commandant. Didi was offered the position of "civilian specialist." They had two aqualungs and a bit of space in the office of the Toulon harbormaster. From this modest reality, they "neglected no opportunity to make ourselves known as a powerful bureau of the Marine Nationale," Jacques joked.

Once again, Jacques and Simone rented a villa in Sanary. This one stood on a hillside overlooking the dazzling Mediterranean. Jacques dove every day with his friends. He was teaching his sons, ages seven and five, to dive. And the children of his brother, Pierre-Antoine, were staying with him, completing the large and carefree group. Jacques felt he had the perfect life.

CLEANING UP THE WAR MESS

The Undersea Research Group lacked equipment, however. Jacques, who somehow usually managed to get what he wanted, quickly found he needed money. The men soon had trucks, motorcycles, and three boats: a launch named *L'Esquillade,* a larger launch called the *VP-8,* and "our biggest equipment *coup,*" according to Jacques, an oceangoing diving boat called the *Albatross.* "We forgot duty hours as we rigged our ship," Jacques said.

Three petty officers joined them: Maurice Fargues, Jean Pinard, and Guy Morandière. Didi put the newcomers through a rigorous diving course, and soon they were expert divers. The Undersea Research Group was complete.

Although the men often felt like happy beach bums, they did dangerous and difficult work every day. Many French harbors, including the one at Toulon and others nearby, were blocked by ships sunk during the war. Even worse, live mines, set to explode on contact, still floated near the surface of the water. All this dangerous debris needed to be cleared.

One of the group's first assignments was clearing the lanes around Porquerolles Island near Toulon. Jacques questioned local fishermen about mines in the area, and they produced a chart marked with a safe lane.

The "safe" lane did not turn out to be very safe, however. As *L'Esquillade* ran down it at full speed in fading evening light, Jacques saw the spiked antennae of a mine passing by within inches of the launch. "I slowed down and posted lookouts," he said. "The bow lookout called out mine after mine."

Once the group had survived locating the mines, they donned their aqualungs and submerged. Disarming a mine is tricky work. Any error in judgment, any slip in handling, can be fatal. After Jacques's divers disarmed a mine, another boat would come along to retrieve it.

One of the worst jobs the group handled involved a

barge sunk just off a main shipping lane. The wreck was in shallow water and could be seen clearly, but it was still a nuisance. A demolition team sent to blow it up noticed some strange objects in the wreck and called in Jacques's group to investigate.

Jacques, Philippe, and Didi submerged and found the wreck filled with curious metal cylinders. They swam around, scraping algae off the cylinders to get a better look at them. Suddenly, Didi grabbed Jacques by the arm and pulled him toward the surface. "I recognize them now," Didi said when the two were well away from the wreck. The cylinders turned out to be "some of the most fiendish mines the Nazis had evolved," according to Jacques. They could be triggered not only by contact but also by sound, pressure, or magnetic waves. "There were twenty tons of high explosive down there waiting," said Jacques. Nothing could be done but rope off the wreck and wait for the sea to corrode the triggering mechanisms. Only then could the explosives be removed safely.

Another project, suggested to the navy by Jacques, was a film to show the public how a submarine lays mines. Jacques had the submarine, the *Rubis*, fire an unarmed torpedo so he could film the action. The result was a short documentary called *A Dive of the Rubis*. The film's viewers were amazed by Jacques's footage of something never before seen on film—a torpedo hurtling by.

With each dive, the group learned more, often at

great personal risk. The men were now diving to depths of 250 feet. One dive nearly cost them their lives, and it wasn't even in the ocean.

CAVE DIVING

Near the town of Avignon, France, a famous natural spring known as the Fountain of Vaucluse burbles from the bottom of a peaceful, seemingly bottomless pool. The spring is always quietly active, but in springtime, for five weeks, the water flows furiously, overflowing the pool and flooding the adjacent River Sorgue near the city of Sorgue. Then it subsides. The mysterious phenomenon occurs every year.

Someone suggested to the navy that the Undersea Research Group explore the spring and find out why it surged every year. In short order, the divers found themselves at the base of the limestone cliff where the Fountain of Vaucluse emerges into its pool.

They had brought along aqualungs and a brand-new diesel-powered air compressor for filling their tanks with air. Simone had come along to watch, although she was worried about the whole venture and did not want them to dive. Many local people had also turned out to see what the group would find.

Maurice Fargues was the surface commander, Jacques and Didi the first divers. As Jacques and Didi descended into the pool, they carried a rope attached to Maurice. The trio had worked out a series of signals. If Jacques or Didi gave one tug, Maurice should tighten the rope. Three tugs meant let out more rope. Six meant Maurice should haul them up as fast as he could.

Jacques and Didi quickly discovered that the Fountain of Vaucluse was flowing from an underground, flooded cave. They dove into it and began following it as it plunged deeper into the earth. As they descended down shafts and through connecting caves, a familiar sensation hit them: the first signs of rapture of the deep.

Rapture of the deep is a dangerous effect caused by the nitrogen in air. When people breath in nitrogen under normal conditions, it is harmless. But at great depths, nitrogen accumulates in a diver's bloodstream. The greater the depth—and the longer a diver remains there—the more nitrogen accumulates. The accumulation causes deadly changes in a person's nervous system. Divers suffering from rapture of the deep experience a drugged feeling. They seem oblivious to the dangers around them and make deadly mistakes in judgment, such as taking off their air tanks.

Jacques was familiar with the sensations of rapture of the deep. But he couldn't believe that rapture of the deep could be affecting them. Didi and he had been in the water for just a few minutes, and they'd only descended 90 feet. Besides, this feeling was different. Instead of feeling pleasantly confident, the divers felt awful. Their heads ached and their vision blurred. The cold was overpowering.

At the Fountain of Vaucluse in southern France, left, *Jacques and his diving team nearly died from carbon monoxide poisoning.*

Jacques was puzzled but decided to continue. The pair followed the cave's twists and turns until they had traveled about 400 feet from their starting point. They were 200 feet underground. Jacques felt drugged, as if he had no initiative. Didi, who was more affected, began to lose control of his jaw. His mouthpiece slipped from his teeth, and he started swallowing water.

Didi began to lose consciousness. Jacques was rational enough to know that they had to go back. But how? In Jacques's fuzzy state, he had forgotten the signals. "I could not swim to the surface, carrying . . . Dumas," he remembered thinking. He decided to climb the rope.

But when Jacques started to climb, his tugs on the rope felt like a signal to Maurice. Three tugs, and Maurice let out more rope. Jacques tried again, and the new tugs were interpreted as more signals for rope. Jacques watched in dismay as more and more rope came down. In less than a minute, Maurice Fargues let down 400 feet of rope. "I dropped the rope like an enemy," Jacques remembered. "I would have to climb the tunnel slope like an Alpinist. . . . dragged down by the weight of Dumas."

Luckily, dragging Didi somehow made Jacques's brain click into action. "The shock turned my mind to the rope again, and I received a last-minute remembrance of our signals: six tugs meant pull everything up. I grabbed the line and jerked it, confident that I could count to six."

Jacques felt the rope tighten and held on. As the two men were drawn upward, Jacques could see a faint triangle of green light overhead. In less than a minute, Maurice had hauled them out of the pool.

Later, Maurice told Jacques that he had felt only a faint vibration in the rope. It wasn't a real signal. Still, he had felt uneasy and pulled them up anyway. Even if Jacques got mad at him, Maurice had figured, "What do I risk? A bawling out?"

As Jacques struggled to recover, Didi lay on his stomach on the ground beside the pool and vomited. Jacques looked around and realized Simone was not at the pool. Saying she couldn't stand the strain, she had fled to a café in town, ordered the most potent drink she could, and waited there until someone came and told her the divers were safe.

What had gone wrong? As the group drove back to Toulon, they tried to figure out what had happened. A chance comment by Didi gave Jacques a flash of intuition. "Didi said, 'Narcotic effects aren't the only cause of diving accidents. There are social and subjective fears, the air you breathe. . . . ' I jumped at the idea. 'The air you breathe!' I said. 'Let's run a lab test on the air left in the lungs.'"

A quick test revealed that their new diesel-powered air compressor had been sucking in its own exhaust and filling their air tanks with the fumes. They had been breathing deadly carbon monoxide—in near lethal doses.

Although the group did further cave diving in Chartres and Estramar, they never returned to the Fountain of Vaucluse.

A Dear Price To Pay

Jacques and the other members of the Undersea Research Group were still interested in exploring just how deep humans could dive. In the summer of 1947, they began a series of deepwater tests.

The ever present threat of rapture of the deep made safety the first concern. As a precaution, a rope was tied around the diver's waist so that he could signal his condition to the crew on deck. A safety man waited, fully suited up, ready to dive in immediately should the diver experience any difficulties.

To determine the depth of a dive, the group dropped a weighted line called a shotline with boards attached at intervals. A diver then descended as deep as he felt comfortable, signed the closest board, and came to the surface. When the shotline was hauled out, the depth of the board he'd signed showed the depth of his dive.

By fall, Jacques had managed to descend 297 feet. That gave him the world's record for independent diving. Still, the group wondered about going deeper. As Jacques explained, "We went lower because that was the only way to learn more about the drunken effect, and to sample individual reaction on what aqualung work could be done in severe depths."

One day Maurice Fargues was the diver, Jean Pinard his safety man. Maurice, who was in the best physical shape of all the divers, jumped in and disappeared. On deck, Jacques and the others received constant tugs on Maurice's rope. All was well. Suddenly the tugs stopped. Jean plunged over the side immediately while the crew frantically hauled in the rope.

Jean found Maurice at the 150-foot level. To Jean's horror, Maurice was hanging limply from the rope, his mouthpiece dangling from his mouth. With the crew hauling and Jean helping, they managed to get Maurice out of the water in less than a minute. They worked for twelve hours trying to revive Maurice, but he was dead, drowned by rapture of the deep.

When the shotline was raised, the crew found Maurice Fargues's name on a board that had been 396 feet deep. "Fargues gave his life a hundred feet below our greatest penetrations," Jacques later wrote.

Maurice's death stunned the group. Jacques especially was inconsolable. As much as he loved exploring new frontiers, the death of one of his men was too dear a price. Jacques reconsidered all the group's safety procedures. He set the extreme boundary for independent compressed-air diving at 300 feet—the deepest dive he himself had ever safely made.

Jacques's ship Calypso *took him and his crew around the globe exploring the ocean world.*

Chapter **SEVEN**

CALYPSO

BY THE LATE **1940**S, JACQUES WAS WELL ESTAB-
lished as an underwater explorer. He was respected by
oceanographers and other scientists, inventors, and
photographers the world over. In addition, the
aqualung was being sold commercially. Ordinary people were beginning to dive.

In 1948, Jacques glimpsed another possibility for exploring the ocean's greatest depths. A Swiss physicist
named Auguste Piccard had developed a *bathyscaphe*,
a Greek word for "deep boat." Piccard's bathyscaphe
could dive twenty-five times deeper than ordinary sub-
marines.

Delayed by World War II, the maiden voyage of the
bathyscaphe took place in 1948. Jacques and the rest

of the Undersea Research Group watched as the bathyscaphe descended an incredible 4,000 feet—and returned safely. There were a few kinks to work out. It capsized once it was back on the surface. Even so, Jacques was ecstatic about the possibilities.

For the time being, however, Jacques and the Undersea Research Group were still using hand-me-down navy ships and rented boats. For years, Jacques had dreamed of his own ship, fully equipped for oceanographic research. His friends laughed, telling him to become an admiral, since that was the only way the navy was going to give him a ship like that. If Jacques wanted a larger ship, he'd have to buy one.

TRANSFORMING CALYPSO

One day, as Jacques told the story, he and Simone sat down at their kitchen table and began looking through their address book, thinking that someone listed might be able to help them finance a ship. They found the name of a wealthy philanthropist, Loel Guiness, whom they'd recently met during an evening out with friends. When Jacques contacted Guiness, Guiness was so impressed with Jacques's ideas that he offered to pay for a ship and any refitting needed.

One problem remained. Jacques still had responsibilities to the French navy. But he had always been adept at dealing with the navy bureaucracy. It took a lot of talking, but he did get three months' leave from the navy to search for a ship.

In 1950, on the island of Malta, Jacques found his ship: *Calypso*. During the war, *Calypso* had been used to find floating mines, but the ship could easily be re-modeled as an expedition vessel. *Calypso* was 140 feet long, weighed 360 tons, and could roll along at 11.5 miles per hour (10.5 knots). A naval architect pro-nounced *Calypso* sound, and Jacques had the ship taken to Antibes for refitting.

The next step was making *Calypso* into a state-of-the-art research vessel. In addition to funds from Guiness, the Cousteaus also put their own money into the project (Simone even sold some valuable antique jewelry to raise money). Simone's father asked his friends for donations. Manufacturers lent or gave equipment. The navy lent a ship's radio.

Jacques, Philippe, and Didi had often brainstormed about the features such a ship should have, and they added many of them now. They put a diving well through the ship's hull so divers could enter the water easily from inside the ship. They built an observation deck high atop *Calypso*, where crew members could scan the distant horizon. And they added an underwa-ter observation chamber. Like a steel bubble on the ship's bow, eight feet below the water line, it had five round windows that made it easy to look around as the ship cruised.

Finally, the refitting crew painted *Calypso* white. The night Jacques and Simone were to leave together on *Calypso's* first expedition—November 24, 1951—they watched their bright boat glisten under the harbor searchlights, their own eyes shining.

EXPLORING A NICE HOT BATHTUB

Calypso pulled away from the twinkling lights of Toulon, headed out across the Mediterranean toward the Red Sea. Sailing with Jacques and Simone were Philippe and Didi. The Cousteau boys were away at school. Jacques, who had no formal scientific training himself, had also asked a number of research scientists to join the expedition. Among the crew were experts in ocean biology, geology, and hydrology (the study of the chemistry and processes of water).

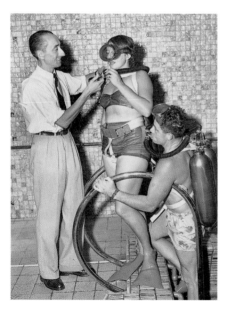

Jacques and volunteers from the U.S. Navy demonstrate the aqualung for the press in the 1950s.

Everyone aboard called each other "professor" or "doctor"—unless a person really held that title. Then he was called *"monsieur"* (sir).

There was not enough money to pay for a complete crew, so everybody pitched in to wash dishes, stand watches, and do other chores. Simone had charge of the sonar, a device for detecting objects underwater. The sonar charted a profile of the seafloor on a roll of paper as *Calypso* plowed ahead. At one point, Simone noted a depth of 16,500 feet—a startling discovery, since the recorded depth in that area was 14,500 feet.

Crew harmony was one of Jacques's top priorities. The crew joked together often. During one meal, *Calypso* was rolling and swaying in heavy waves so much that people were falling over the dinner table, which struck them all as hilarious. Everyone worked well together, but Jacques was clearly in charge. Wearing a jaunty red wool cap, Captain Cousteau manned the helm or strode the decks, monitoring everything.

In the Red Sea ("a nice hot bathtub full of sharks," Jacques joked), *Calypso* left the superhighway of oil freighters to cruise among little-charted coral reefs and islands. As the crew dove, they encountered many rare plants and animals. They spent hours every day collecting and cataloging the life-forms. In fact, they discovered so many new species that they had trouble naming all of them.

They filmed everything they saw. They were constantly trying out different cameras and experimenting with new lighting techniques. Ever since Jacques and Didi had discovered the astounding colors of the deep sea, Jacques had wanted to capture that color on film. He realized that funding for future expeditions of the *Calypso* would depend on breathtaking films.

And the underwater world was breathtaking. Jacques described one coral wall as "a splendid tilted forest" where "big, transparent jellyfish dragged along, pulsating drowsily" and "moray eels glowered from crevices and bared their teeth to impress us," while "humpbacked sea snails traveled their winding ways."

Jacques pressed his mask close against the coral "like a child at a candy-store window" and discovered tiny worms and hairy crabs and flowering slugs in miniature crevices. Overhead, he saw sharks, "one or two in every direction, and now they were closing in. Some swam straight toward me with vacant eyes," he wrote, "and then withdrew."

One night, while watching from *Calypso's* observation bubble, Jacques spied a swarm of sea creatures too tiny to identify swimming in the ship's light. A large animal hovered in the darkness just outside the halo of light, perhaps, as Jacques said, "waiting for the light to go out before raiding the careless fry dancing in the night club."

RAISING MONEY—AND SUNKEN CARGO

By the end of the expedition, the group had gathered an impressive amount of new information about the

Jacques and Calypso's divers, like the one above, were astounded by the brilliant colors of fish, animals, and plants surrounding them when they shone light on the undersea world to make their films.

Red Sea. Jacques headed to the United States to publicize *Calypso's* mission and to raise money. In Washington, D.C., he met with Gilbert Grosvenor, the president of the National Geographic Society. In New York City, Jacques talked to executives of the CBS television network, trying to persuade them to sponsor three ninety-minute films.

People were interested in Captain Cousteau and the

crew of *Calypso*. That fall, the National Geographic Society offered to sponsor Jacques's next mission. With such a prestigious organization backing him, Jacques soon gained additional funding from the French navy and other organizations.

In the summer of 1952, acting on a tip Didi had received from a fellow diver, Jacques took *Calypso* to the island of Grand Congloué ten miles off the coast near Marseilles. The diver had described some "old jars" sunk below the base of the island. Jacques and Didi suspected there might be a shipwreck nearby.

They found the ship—well camouflaged under pebbles, fallen boulders, and other debris—at a depth of about 140 feet. Archaeologists who examined the old jars declared them to be amphorae—cargo jars—made in Greece in the third century B.C. No doubt the ancient ship, while on its way to Marseilles to sell a cargo of wine, had rammed the island and sunk.

The shipwreck was a remarkable find, and archaeologists around the world were thrilled. Jacques developed a special TV camera to film the underwater artifacts. After several months, he took *Calypso* on to other work but assigned a crew, including diver Albert Falco, to stay with the wreck and excavate it. The crew knew they were facing a long job, so they built a little village on the island where they could live and called it Port Calypso.

Digging through the debris, winching the ship's fragile cargo out of the water, and filming everything took five years in all. Jacques kept track of the group's progress and visited Port Calypso regularly. One rare day, he got a treat—a taste of wine, 2,200 years old, found in one of the old jars.

Jacques Cousteau became a household name by producing films of a world never before seen by television viewers.

Chapter **EIGHT**

BOOK AND FILM FAME

IN **1953, JACQUES PUBLISHED HIS FIRST BOOK,** *The Silent World*, written with Frédéric Dumas. It was an instant success. Drawn from Jacques's and Didi's logs, the book's personal writing style, as well as the wonders and exploits it described, touched a responsive chord with the American public. By the end of the year, *The Silent World* had sold nearly half a million copies. Jacques was earning a great deal of money, and he and the crew of *Calypso* were famous.

In some ways, the publicity was a mixed blessing. Funding for *Calypso*'s expeditions became easier to get, but the sudden rush of attention was also difficult to handle. Jacques's small, tightly knit crew was used to hanging out together in remote locations. Suddenly, every place they went they were mobbed and asked for autographs. They felt overwhelmed. Even Jacques—who seemed to instinctively draw the spotlight toward himself—was taken aback.

Calypso's next expedition was funded in part by the British Petroleum Company, which wanted to analyze underwater rock samples in the Persian Gulf to determine where to drill for oil.

In January 1954, *Calypso* departed for the Gulf to collect the samples. Although gathering rocks wasn't precisely what Jacques wanted to do, British Petroleum paid well for the work, and Jacques was always on the lookout for money to help pay for more undersea research.

For two months the crew did backbreaking work, chiseling rock from ledges 150 feet deep. Sharks and venomous sea snakes posed a constant threat. The water was bone-chilling cold, while the temperature above water was unbearably hot. Everyone was relieved when the samples were ready to send to British Petroleum. Then *Calypso* headed to the Indian Ocean and the eastern coast of Africa to explore. For nearly four months, Jacques and the crew swam and filmed. In the waters of the Indian Ocean, where sharks roam, safety was a constant concern. The crew used protective cages and always worked in teams. "The better acquainted we become with sharks, the less we know them," Jacques later wrote. "One can never tell what a shark is going to do."

A NEW SPORT

The aqualung fundamentally altered diving in two ways. First, it provided a reliable breathing mechanism that divers could easily carry with them and use without thought. Second, it could be easily manufactured in versions that ordinary people could afford.

Air Liquide (the French natural gas company that employed both Émile Gagnan and Jacques's father-in-law) put the aqualung into commercial production. But so many people wanted to own an aqualung that the company could not keep up with demand. Competitors began to produce imitations with slight alterations. An entire industry was born, and scuba diving became a new, widely available sport. Each year in the 1990s, an estimated five hundred thousand divers were certified in the United States alone.

Scuba lessons have grown in popularity since the 1950s. These scuba students are learning how to use the aqualung in 1956.

By the time *Calypso* headed back to the Mediterranean, her crew members were exhausted. Jacques
decided everyone could relax on the way home. They
started a card game in the Gulf of Suez, and it didn't
end until they pulled into the harbor of Toulon.

THE SILENT WORLD

For several months during 1954 and 1955, *Calypso*
was in dry dock for overhauling. The crew's quarters
were revamped, and all equipment was checked and
checked again. The team purchased new lighting
equipment, cameras, and film. Jacques also hired several more photographers and cinematographers. By
March 1955, *Calypso* was a floating movie studio.

All the preparations meant Jacques had what he
needed to produce a full-length documentary film that
would also have the name *The Silent World*. Jacques
planned to use some of his earnings from his book to
fund the film. Louis Malle, a talented young French
filmmaker, was one of *Calypso*'s new crew members
and would help get the footage needed for *The Silent
World*.

To begin making the new film, Jacques and the crew
of *Calypso* sailed through the Red Sea, then journeyed
south to the Indian Ocean and the Seychelles Islands
and Assumption Island off the eastern coast of Africa.
By now, the Cousteaus made their home aboard *Calypso*. Simone could often be found standing at the
rail. Jean-Michel and Philippe, who were teenagers,

had become enthusiastic divers and often joined the diving teams.

When *Calypso* finally returned to Toulon, it had covered 13,700 miles. Jacques and Louis began sorting through the hours of film they had shot, looking for footage they could use in *The Silent World*. The two disagreed about how the film should be made. Louis preferred an artistic approach. Jacques emphasized the adventure involved. In the end, they compromised. The opening scene of the film—which shows a froth of air bubbles disturbing quiet blue water—was Louis's idea. The next scene—divers climbing up the ladder to *Calypso*'s deck—came from Jacques.

Jacques's first well-known film, The Silent World, *showed divers circling around sunken ships while schools of fish flashed by them.*

The audience of The Silent World *could finally investigate brilliantly colored fish as closely as the divers could.*

The Silent World, codirected by Jacques-Yves Cousteau and Louis Malle, debuted at the 1956 Cannes Film Festival. The audience was astonished by the camerawork and the stunning undersea images it revealed. The film went on to win the festival's highest award, the Palme d'Or. One year later, in Hollywood, the film won an Oscar for best documentary.

Jacques's earlier films were beautiful and technically complex, but his viewing audience had been very small. *The Silent World* marked the beginning of his mainstream professional film career. Developing his own state-of-the-art equipment and filming techniques, he went on to make more than seventy full-length films and television specials. Many won Emmys, Oscars, Palmes d'Or, and other awards. By 1957, "Jacques Cousteau" was a household name. People around the world had heard of the tall, witty Frenchman and his ship *Calypso*.

Jacques was still in the French navy, however, where his film success meant little. Still a captain at age forty-seven, Jacques was the lowest ranked among his former classmates at the naval academy—the rest had risen through the ranks. Jacques decided he should resign. Resigning was a difficult decision, but both Jacques and Simone felt it was the best thing to do. Living on *Calypso* for several years had changed them. They had little use for the navy's routine, and both felt that *Calypso* had become their true home. Although by retiring Jacques gave up his title as captain in the navy, he was still captain of *Calypso*. People continued to call him Captain Cousteau for the rest of his life.

A NEW JOB

A perfect opportunity presented itself almost immediately. Less than one hundred miles away, Prince Rainier of Monaco, a free diver himself, was looking for a new director to head the well-respected Oceanographic Institute of Monaco. In many ways, the position was an honorary one. Jacques would still be free to conduct his own business and explore with

Calpyso. He accepted the job at once.

As *Calypso* continued voyaging through oceans and along coastlines all over the world, Jacques made notes of everything the crew saw and did. His descriptions were detailed, precise, and vivid. In *The Living Sea,* a book he published in 1956 with a *Calypso* crew member, James Dugan, Jacques told of watching a "living reef" of twenty thousand dolphins leaping along the surface of the Indian Ocean. "The tails were clearing twelve to fifteen feet," he wrote. To Jacques, it seemed as if the dolphins swam with "no apparent destination, given up to some titanic, collective joy." The people watching from *Calypso* "shouted like children and bet on leaps."

From *Calypso*'s underwater observation chamber, the sight was even more astonishing. The water was packed with submerged dolphins. Dolphins streamed alongside the ship or swam up to the windows to look inside. Others "sped straight up from the deep," Jacques wrote, "threw themselves into a sort of secondary rocket-booster stage in front of the windows, and shot through the glittering ceiling."

Jacques continued to invent and develop the machines he needed to learn more about life in the ocean and to film it. In 1959, Jacques built a bathyscaphe. He had looked forward to owning his own bathyscaphe ever since he had joined the test of Auguste Piccard's bathyscaphe eleven years earlier. Jacques's version, a two-man "diving saucer," became a standard

Jacques built several bathyscaphes in the 1950s and 1960s. He kept improving his "diving saucers" to explore the sea for long periods of time. This bathyscaphe was built in 1965.

piece of equipment aboard *Calypso*. Jacques's diving saucer could stay submerged for six hours and descend to 1,146 feet. At that depth, "everything is to be discovered," as Jacques noted in his logbook. In the diving saucer, *Calypso*'s crew could carefully study the layers of life in the ocean from the surface downward. Jacques filmed jellyfish, swimming worms, and other deepwater life no one had ever seen before. Riding along and looking through the portholes of the snug saucer was like gliding through the Milky Way on a beautiful summer night.

That summer, Jacques took *Calypso* to New York

Calypso's crew, shown here celebrating a record-setting voyage in 1956, included Jacques, above left, in white shirt, *his wife Simone,* center, in white cap, *and his son Philippe,* center, in baseball cap.

City to take part in the first International Oceanographic Congress. The ship was greeted with sirens and waterworks as it came into the city's harbor. Thousands of journalists, scientists, officials, and other visitors toured the ship. Jacques and the crew were treated like stars.

By the early 1960s, Jacques's fame was at its peak. His name and face were everywhere, even on the cover of *Time* magazine. Thanks to the aqualung, more than one million Americans had taken up scuba diving. President John F. Kennedy presented Jacques with the National Geographic Society's Gold Medal during a ceremony in the Rose Garden at the White House in 1961. On the back of the medal were the words "To earthbound man he gave the key to the silent world."

Jacques's bathyscaphe evolved into three versions of Conshelf
(continental shelf station). Aquanauts lived in and conducted
underwater research for up to two months in the steel houses.

Chapter **NINE**

CONSHELF AND
TV DEALS

As THE **1960**s BEGAN, THE SPACE RACE WAS ON.
John Glenn orbited the Earth, Americans longed to
get to the moon, and scientists speculated that one
day people could travel and live in space.

In the first photographs taken by astronauts, Earth
looked so blue. People could clearly see that nearly
seventy percent of our planet is covered by water.
Jacques started thinking about those vast blue regions
in the same way scientists were thinking about space.
If humans could travel and live in space someday, perhaps they could also travel and live underwater.

To begin, Jacques wanted to build one underwater
living station. The best site would be a continental
shelf, the part of a continent that lies underwater

along its shoreline, extending seaward for a few miles. Compared to the rest of the ocean, the continental shelf is in shallow water.

Once again, Jacques's amazing ability to win support helped him turn his dreams into reality. He got financial backing from the French oil industry and made plans to sell films of life in the underwater station to defray some of the costs.

Before long, Conshelf (short for "continental shelf station") was ready. It was a watertight cylinder about the size of a large bedroom. Jacques had it anchored in 27 feet of water in the Mediterranean near Marseilles. Radio and video monitors linked it to the surface. Inside were all the comforts of home, including champagne (although at Conshelf's depth, the champagne had no bubbles since the water pressure kept the bubbles from frothing).

In September 1962, two "aquanauts," Albert Falco and Claude Wesly, entered the Conshelf station ready to stay for a week. Life underwater was hardly dull. Albert and Claude left the station every day to perform experiments, dive, and explore. They built fish corrals and cement-block fish houses because Jacques was intrigued with the idea of underwater fish ranches. And they had visitors—Jacques and several journalists and doctors.

When the two men returned to the surface, they were in excellent condition, showing no ill effects. Claude told everyone he'd gotten so used to being underwater that he almost forgot he was wearing air tanks during dives. Albert reminded people of the wreck off the island of Grand Congloué. "We worked several years at a hundred and forty feet. . . , " he had written in his log. "If only we'd had a house on the floor [of the sea] for that job!"

Jacques was excited about the results of Conshelf. He was convinced that Conshelf would be an advancement for human civilization. Jacques even believed that, if generations of humans spent enough time living underwater in places like Conshelf, humans might evolve further and truly become the "menfish" of his dreams.

Many people, however, scoffed at those ideas. Diving to great depths for short periods was understandable. But living underwater? Some people thought Jacques had gone too far. He was confusing reality with science fiction.

The following year, a second station, Conshelf II, was anchored in the Red Sea near Port Sudan, in Sudan. Conshelf II had two chambers. The first, called Starfish House, was located at a depth of 30 feet. The second, Deep Cabin, was 74 feet deep.

Five aquanauts lived in Starfish House for four weeks. Two lived in Deep Cabin for one week. Deep Cabin had several technical problems. Cables broke, it leaked, and it had a tendency to slide along the ledge where it was anchored. Each time it slid, surface cranes and cables had to reposition it.

Unlike Starfish House, which had an atmosphere of air, Deep Cabin had an atmosphere that was half air and half helium. Jacques theorized that divers, acclimated to a helium-rich atmosphere in a deep diving station, would be able to dive deeper than was possible when beginning from the surface. The aquanauts of Deep Cabin proved him right. They made dives to 360 feet and returned safely.

As with all of Jacques's diving expeditions, a film crew recorded everything on Conshelf II. The resulting film, *World without Sun,* won an Oscar in 1964 for best documentary film.

Jacques's next station, Conshelf III, was ready in September 1965. Anchored in the Mediterranean at a depth of 296 feet, it was Jacques's most ambitious underwater living experiment. Six men spent twenty-two days living inside the globe-shaped structure while 150 technicians and a dozen ships provided support from the surface.

One of the aquanauts in Conshelf III was twenty-four-year-old Philippe Cousteau, Jacques's younger son. Philippe served as camerman. Even as a child, Philippe had shared Jacques's fascination with diving, which delighted Jacques. The fact that Philippe had been included as a member of the Conshelf III team revealed how much Jacques trusted his diving skills.

When the aquanauts surfaced after nearly a month of underwater life, the experiment was considered a great success. "We had proved our point that man

This promotional poster for Cousteau's film World without Sun *portrayed scenes from the "oceanauts'" adventures.*

can occupy and exploit the sea bottom," Jacques wrote. "Perhaps most significant of all, we had begun to breed a new...sense of confidence. Our young men began to think into, to feel, the undersea environment."

Jacques hoped to continue building Conshelf stations, anchoring them at increasing depths. But Conshelf III was the last of the projects. The price tag was astronomical—the Conshelf III chamber alone had cost more than $700,000. Jacques had counted on the

Philippe Cousteau was a vital part of Calypso's crew and a prized colleague of his father.

sale of the Conshelf III film to help with expenses. But he was unable to line up a distributor because the helium the aquanauts breathed had such an odd side effect: it made their voices squeaky. They sounded ridiculous.

The Conshelf projects had broken new frontiers. Yet Jacques abandoned his dream of living underwater. In a 1996 interview, Jacques was asked, "You experimented with living under the sea for long periods of time. Is there a future to that, do you think?" Jacques responded, "No, none." Jacques had always dreamed of "menfish," but it was not to be. For now, he was satisfied with what had been learned.

THE UNDERSEA WORLD OF JACQUES COUSTEAU

The failure to find a distributor for the Conshelf III film was disappointing to Jacques. But disappointment once again opened new doors for him. The Conshelf III film footage did become a National Geographic television special, produced by David Wolper and narrated by Orson Welles. Broadcast in

Jacques's films earned him respect and fame as a filmmaker. He began producing television specials for the National Geographic Society and for ABC network in 1966.

April 1966, the program led to an extraordinary $4.2 million deal with the American Broadcasting Corporation (ABC).

All three of the major American television networks had been interested in broadcasting specials on the Cousteau expeditions. People loved to watch them. Because Jacques produced his films in a straightforward, factual style, they were consistently placed in the documentary category when awards were given. But Jacques held a different view. "We are not documentary. We are adventure films, " he said. "If you notice, there are hardly any 'facts' in [my films] at all. . . . As soon as you are specific, the poetry disappears."

The $4.2 million contract with ABC came after weeks of talking. Philippe worked alongside Jacques to negotiate the deal. Jacques was to produce three one-hour specials a year for four years—twelve specials in all. The new series, to be called *The Undersea World of Jacques Cousteau,* would give Jacques the financial stability to plan the expeditions he wanted—and plan them far in advance.

Jacques had formed his own film company, Sharks Associated, and it would shoot all the material. The postproduction work would be handled by David Wolper Productions in Los Angeles. Philippe was to be the mediator between Sharks Associated and David Wolper Productions. He would live in Los Angeles, but he would have to travel constantly between New York, Paris, and wherever *Calypso* was at the moment.

A FAMILY BUSINESS

With Jacques's fame growing and his ventures expanding, Jacques was no longer just one person, happily diving in the Mediterranean. He was a multimillion-dollar industry. Both Jean-Michel and Philippe were involved in their father's work, although not to the same degree. Jean-Michel was interested in many different things and wasn't as focused as Philippe on Jacques's projects.

Since Conshelf III, Jacques had relied more and more on Philippe in business matters. In fact, Philippe had become a constant presence at Jacques's side. Many observers outside the family assumed that Philippe was being groomed to run the Cousteau business empire. Philippe's charm was apparent. He seemed destined to become as accomplished and famous as his father, perhaps even more so.

Or so it seemed. While Philippe had been in New York for the negotiations with ABC, he had fallen in love with a beautiful American model named Janice Sullivan. When the deal was done and the Cousteaus were back in Paris, Philippe announced to his parents that he and Jan wanted to get married.

Jacques and Simone were horrified. Janice couldn't speak French, and she had never even heard of Jacques Cousteau. Besides, the Cousteaus didn't want their twenty-six-year-old son to marry anyone yet. Jacques had other plans for Philippe.

Despite the objections of Jacques and Simone, in

January 1967, Philippe married Jan in Paris. Neither Jacques nor Simone attended the wedding. They did offer their new daughter-in-law a wedding present—a six-week crash course in French.

After the wedding, the air was distinctly chilly between Jacques and Philippe. There was work to be done, though. Philippe began filming the migration of gray whales along the California coast. Jacques took the newly refurbished *Calypso* out of its homeport of Monaco for an open-ended expedition.

Filming for the new television series was an emotional roller coaster. The footage had to be exciting, yet exact. The first show in the series would be titled "Sharks." Filming the shark sequences was particularly stressful as the crew strove to get dramatic shots without getting themselves killed.

In the winter of 1968, millions of viewers began watching Jacques's new TV series. *Calypso* was traveling in the Caribbean. Production was proceeding on schedule, but the relationship between Jacques and Philippe had deteriorated. Philippe wanted more responsibility, while Jacques complained that Philippe would have to work harder to earn it. In 1969, Philippe quit to start his own film company.

Meanwhile, Jean-Michel had become more active in his father's film production business. People began to assume that Jean-Michel was the logical choice to take over the family enterprises.

As Jacques's sons were struggling in their relation-

Jean-Michel Cousteau became involved in his father's television specials in the late 1960s. He and Cousteau traveled both sea and land to show viewers different forms of life.

ships with their father, other people seemed to be growing more and more fond of Jacques. In his native France, he consistently ranked near the top in polls asking who should be president. He was nearly always first in polls asking people to name their most beloved person. It seemed people couldn't help but admire the daring captain in the red cap, pictured against the background of the wild blue sea.

All the while, Jacques said nothing publicly about the roles of his two sons. At times, he even seemed to enjoy the uncertainty and tension he was creating.

*The Cousteaus and the Calypso crew in Monaco in 1970,
around the time Cousteau became more concerned about
protecting the environment*

Chapter **TEN**

A VISION
SHARED

IN THE **1960**S, JACQUES HAD TALKED ABOUT THE sea as an exploitable resource. In the 1970s, he began to talk more and more about the importance of protecting the sea. The sea gives people food, minerals, and other resources. It moderates air temperature, helping to keep the Earth from becoming too hot or too cold. And it is the source of rainfall—of life-giving water. People need the oceans in order to live.

Yet the sea was being used as a dump site for silt, sewage, and garbage. In addition, ships carrying oil, chemicals, and radioactive materials sometimes had accidents, which created hazardous spills. As Jacques warned, "The oceans are in danger of dying."

Out of this conviction, in 1973, Jacques founded an

organization dedicated to preserving the fragile ocean environment—the Cousteau Society. Jacques was the society's president and Philippe its vice president, even though the two still had chilly relations. Jean-Michel was also a founding member of the Cousteau Society, but he kept his distance. While fond of their father, both sons found Jacques difficult to work with.

Over the next three years, Jacques and Philippe came to admit that they missed and needed each other. Jean-Michel was an excellent businessman, but he lacked the appeal that Philippe possessed. By 1976, when Jan gave birth to Jacques and Simone's first grandchild, Alexandra, the reconciliation of Jacques and Philippe was complete.

Jacques was increasingly alarmed by the pollution of the world's oceans. Philippe was more concerned about the destruction of wildlife and wild habitats. Both men began using their influence to affect environmental policies, often appearing before the U.S. Congress and international organizations.

In 1976, ABC canceled *The Undersea World of Jacques Cousteau*. The move stunned many since the series was well watched around the world. But Jacques soon agreed to produce two new series for PBS. *Cousteau Odyssey* would cover exploration of the oceans, while *Oasis in Space* would focus on more controversial matters such as world hunger, pollution, and what Jacques called the "primary pollution"— human overpopulation.

THE COUSTEAU SOCIETY

The Cousteau Society is a nonprofit organization dedicated to the preservation of the world's oceans and marine life. Founded by Captain Jacques-Yves Cousteau in 1973, the society is supported solely by its members—150,000 people worldwide in 1999. Francine Cousteau is the society's president.

Although the research ship *Calypso* sank in 1996, the society still conducts expeditions with a second vessel, the *Alcyone,* first put into service in 1985. Sir Peter Blake of New Zealand leads the society's expeditions and its efforts to raise funds for a new ship, *Calypso II.* To learn more about the Cousteau Society or to become a member, contact:

The Cousteau Society
870 Greenbriar Circle, Suite 402
Chesapeake, VA 23320
Phone: (800) 441-4395
E-mail: cousteau@infini.net
Website: http://www.cousteau.org

The Cousteau Society's adventures take place throughout the world. These divers are slicing through the Donau River in eastern Europe for the TV special Cousteau's Rediscovery of the World.

By 1978, the Cousteau Society had several hundred thousand members. It boasted a research and educational center in Norfolk, Virginia, and offices in Los Angeles, California. It was publishing two magazines, *Dolphin Log* for children and *Calypso Log* for adults.

A Sudden Grief

Within the Cousteau business empire, things were running fairly smoothly. Jean-Michel was not actively involved, but Philippe was running studies, expeditions, and film operations. He completed a year-long study of the Mediterranean Sea and began a similar project on the Nile River in Egypt. An expert sailor and pilot, he often flew a PYB (a kind of flying boat, or seaplane) that he had christened the *Flying Calypso*.

In June 1979, Philippe and seven crew members left the Nile in the *Flying Calypso* to fly to Lisbon, Portugal. When the group reached the Tagus River, just outside Lisbon, Philippe looked for a straight, flat stretch of water where he could land. He lightly touched down. The plane bounced a bit off the river's surface, then bounced back onto the water. Suddenly, the plane hit something, flipped over, and broke apart.

With the help of local fishermen, the crew members managed to scramble out. Everyone was relieved— until they realized that Philippe was missing. His body was recovered three days later.

People from around the world flew to Lisbon to attend Philippe's funeral. After a brief service, Philippe was buried at sea. Jan and little Alexandra flew home to Los Angeles, where, a few months later, Jan gave birth to a second child, a boy she named Philippe Pierre Jacques-Yves Cousteau.

Jacques was overwhelmed with grief. Jean-Michel thought Jacques seemed even more inconsolable than Simone. He tried to fill the hole left by Philippe's death. "Dad said to me, 'I need you. I must have your help or else I will quit.' I told him, 'I'm in, don't say another word. It's taken care of.' Once again, I was working for my father."

Jacques began to travel at a frantic pace, flying into one city and giving a speech to a group, then flying on to the next city. Many of his friends believed he was working too hard, keeping the busy schedule in an unsuccessful effort to forget his terrible loss.

Jean-Michel faced a difficult situation. Philippe was a tough act to follow, and Jean-Michel had a different style. Jean-Michel had been away from *Calypso* and his family's enterprises for six years. And working with his father had never been easy. Jacques's distraction and grief made the task even more difficult. But Jean-Michel threw himself into the work of the Cousteau Society with a fierce determination.

Jacques was free to do as he wished. Throughout the 1980s, he supported environmental causes with a wholehearted purpose. He continued to make environmental films and television specials. In 1981 he struck a deal with Ted Turner's cable television network to produce a series called *Rediscovery of the World.* Jacques continued to attract television audiences, but somehow his films no longer startled people into seeing the world anew. His success had spawned so many competitors that nature documentaries had become almost commonplace.

In 1990, at the age of seventy-two, Simone died of cancer. She had been Jacques's wife for more than fifty years and his partner on nearly all his *Calypso* expeditions. Like Philippe, she was buried at sea.

Shortly after Simone's death, Jacques made a startling announcement. For fifteen years, he said, he had maintained a romantic relationship with another woman, Francine Triplet. He had had two children with Francine: a daughter, Diane, born in 1980, and a son, Pierre-Yves, born in 1982. Jacques introduced his second family to the public with photo spreads in French magazines.

Although many people were stunned, most did not condemn Jacques. For decades he had been a remarkably popular person. Besides, in France, people did not consider it unusual that a man would have a girlfriend while being married. In 1991, Jacques and Francine were married.

THE RIGHTS OF FUTURE GENERATIONS

The same year, Jacques also began one of his most ambitious environmental campaigns. He wanted the United Nations to adopt a Bill of Rights for Future

Jacques's second wife, Francine, leads the Cousteau Society.

Generations. The bill would draw attention to the long-range problems of pollution. After all, if people did not act to protect the Earth, their children and grandchildren would have nothing.

Jacques began seeking signatures from members of the Cousteau Society and other environmental organizations and from the general public. Millions of people signed his simple petition. Then he took his case to the United Nations: people around the world were concerned about pollution and wanted it stopped.

A BILL OF RIGHTS FOR FUTURE GENERATIONS

rticle 1
Future generations have a right to an uncontaminated and undamaged Earth and to its enjoyment as the ground of human history, of culture, and of social bonds that make each generation and individual a member of one human family.

Article 2
Each generation, sharing in the estate and heritage of the Earth, has a duty as trustee for future generations to prevent irreversible and irreparable harm to life on Earth and to human freedom and dignity.

Article 3
It is, therefore, the paramount responsibility of each generation to maintain a constantly vigilant and prudential assessment of technological disturbances and modifications adversely affecting life on Earth, the balance of nature, and the evolution of humanity in order to protect the rights of future generations.

Article 4
All appropriate measures, including education, research and legislation, shall be taken to guarantee these rights and to ensure that they not be sacrificed for present expediencies and conveniences.

Article 5
Governments, non-governmental organizations, and individuals are urged, therefore, imaginatively to implement these principles, as if in the very presence of those future generations whose rights we seek to establish and perpetuate.

They wanted a clean planet for future generations. Ambassadors at the United Nations listened carefully and began the long process of considering the bill.

Calypso was still traveling the globe, but more and more, Jacques remained at home with Francine, Diane, and Pierre-Yves. Jacques still spoke often to environmental groups. He appeared before French government committees, wrote letters, and in many other ways served as a senior spokesperson for environmental issues.

Jacques smiles on Calypso in his trademark red cap.

Although Jacques appeared to be blissfully happy with Francine and their children, his personal life was hardly free from trouble. In 1992, Jean-Michel resigned from the Cousteau Society, saying he could no longer work with his father or with Francine.

In 1993 Jacques was appointed to the United Nations High-Level Advisory Board on Sustainable Development. He also agreed to serve as an environmental adviser to the World Bank. That same year, the president of France named Jacques chairman of a newly created Council on the Rights of Future Generations. But in 1995, Jacques resigned in protest of France's nuclear testing in the Pacific.

In January 1996, *Calypso* was struck by a wayward barge in Singapore harbor and sank. Jacques appealed to the public for money to raise and repair *Calypso*. He also wanted twenty million dollars to build a new exploration vessel to be known as *Calypso II*. It was a considerable request. But Jacques had always managed to achieve the seemingly impossible.

This time, however, things were different. In early 1997, Jacques was hospitalized for several months, suffering from a respiratory ailment. On June 15, 1997, he died in his apartment in Paris. He was eighty-seven.

REMEMBERING JACQUES

Around the world, devoted fans, environmentalists, and world leaders mourned the death of Jacques-Yves

Cousteau. U.S. President Bill Clinton wrote, "While we mourn his death, it is far more appropriate that we celebrate his remarkable life and the gifts he gave to all of us." Ted Turner, whose TV network had produced Jacques's latest television films, declared, "I think Captain Cousteau might be the father of the environmental movement."

Many honors had been bestowed on the personable Frenchman. He held honorary degrees from Harvard University, the University of California at Berkeley, Brandeis University, and Rensselaer Polytechnic Institute. He was one of just a few foreign members of America's prestigious National Academy of Sciences. He had been given France's Chevalier de la Legion d'Honneur and the United Nation's International Environmental Prize. To ordinary people, though, it was enough that Jacques had been Captain Cousteau, the beaming man standing on the deck of his ship *Calypso*.

A tremendous tribute to Jacques's efforts came when the United Nations declared 1998 the Year of the Ocean. Scientists, government officials, and environmentalists came together to discuss the future of the world's oceans. The Bill of Rights for Future Generations continued to collect signatures. According to the Cousteau Society, more than eight million signatures had been collected by 1999.

Eventually *Calypso* was raised from Singapore harbor. The ship was taken to La Rochelle, France, where it became a maritime museum. The Cousteau Society

Jacques's relatives bid him good-bye at his memorial service. From left are Pierre-Yves (his son with Francine), Francine, Diane (his daughter with Francine), and Jean-Michel.

still plans to build *Calypso II,* the new research vessel Jacques wanted.

Adventurer, inventor, filmmaker: Jacques had been all of these. Perhaps his greatest legacy is the respect he taught for both the wonder and the necessity of our oceans. Jacques had once crashed his car on a mountain road and, as he lay in the dark, looked up at the stars. "How lucky I was," he had said, "to have seen so many things in my life." Decades later, Jacques had shown others so much. He gave people the chance to glimpse, along with him, the beauty of a silent blue world, pulsing beneath bright stars.

THE LIFE OF COUSTEAU

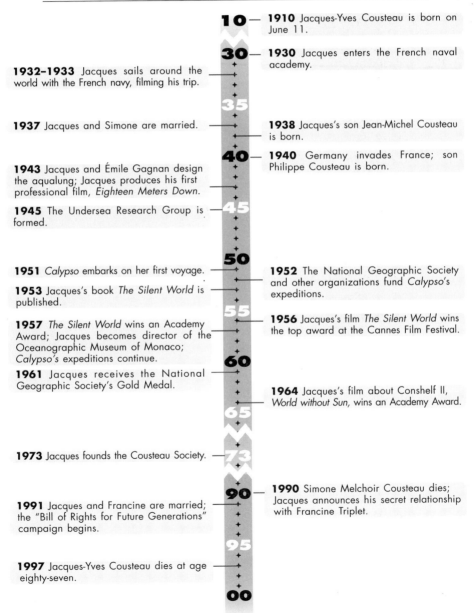

10 — **1910** Jacques-Yves Cousteau is born on June 11.

30 — **1930** Jacques enters the French naval academy.

1932–1933 Jacques sails around the world with the French navy, filming his trip.

35

1937 Jacques and Simone are married.

1938 Jacques's son Jean-Michel Cousteau is born.

40 — **1940** Germany invades France; son Philippe Cousteau is born.

1943 Jacques and Émile Gagnan design the aqualung; Jacques produces his first professional film, *Eighteen Meters Down.*

1945 The Undersea Research Group is formed.

45

50

1951 *Calypso* embarks on her first voyage.

1952 The National Geographic Society and other organizations fund *Calypso's* expeditions.

1953 Jacques's book *The Silent World* is published.

55

1957 *The Silent World* wins an Academy Award; Jacques becomes director of the Oceanographic Museum of Monaco; *Calypso's* expeditions continue.

1956 Jacques's film *The Silent World* wins the top award at the Cannes Film Festival.

60

1961 Jacques receives the National Geographic Society's Gold Medal.

1964 Jacques's film about Conshelf II, *World without Sun*, wins an Academy Award.

65

1973 Jacques founds the Cousteau Society.

73

90 — **1990** Simone Melchoir Cousteau dies; Jacques announces his secret relationship with Francine Triplet.

1991 Jacques and Francine are married; the "Bill of Rights for Future Generations" campaign begins.

95

1997 Jacques-Yves Cousteau dies at age eighty-seven.

00

SOURCES

8 Jacques-Yves Cousteau with Frédéric Dumas, *The Silent World* (Oxford: Clio Press, 1989), 6.
8 Ibid., 7.
9 Ibid.
17 Axel Madsen, *Cousteau* (New York: Beaufort Books, 1986), 18.
25 Cousteau with Dumas, 13.
26 Ibid., 14.
30 Ibid., 15.
33 Ibid.
36 Ibid., 31.
37 Ibid., 17.
39–40 Ibid., 48.
39 Ibid., 4.
43 Ibid., 38.
44 Ibid., 185–186.
45 Ibid., 186.
46 Ibid., 48.
47 Ibid.
48 Ibid., 49.
49 Ibid., 53.
50 Ibid., 54.
54 Ibid., 73.
54 Ibid., 74.
55 Ibid., 74–75.
56 Ibid., 75.
54 Ibid., 78–79.
55 Ibid., 106.
56 Ibid., 110.
63 Captain J.-Y. Cousteau with James Dugan, *The Living Sea* (New York: Harper & Row, 1963), 25.
63 Ibid., 18.
64 Ibid., 19.
64 Ibid., 46.
71–72 Cousteau with Dumas, 154.

76 Cousteau with Dugan, 123.
76 Ibid.
83 Ibid., 324.
84–85 Jacques-Yves Cousteau, *The Ocean World of Jacques Cousteau: Oasis in Space* (New York: The World Publishing Company/Times Mirror, 1972), 127.
84 Jim Motavelli and Susan Elan, "Jacques-Yves Cousteau at 85: The Undersea World of a True Environmental Explorer," *E: The Environmental Magazine*, March 1, 1996.
88 Gerald Jonas, "Jacques Cousteau, Ocean's Impresario, Dies," *New York Times*, June 26, 1997, A1.
93 Ibid.
97 John Brant, "Daddy Dearest," *Outside*, March 1996.
103 CNN Interactive, "Jacques Cousteau Remembered for His 'Common Touch,'" June 25, 1997, <www.cnn.com/WORLD/9706/25/cousteau.obit/index.html>.
104 Madsen, 18.

BIBLIOGRAPHY

Selected Books by Jacques Cousteau
Jacques Cousteau wrote—or wrote with coauthors—more than fifty books. Many were translated and published in more than a dozen languages. Some of his most significant books follow.

Cousteau, Jacques. *The Ocean World*. New York: Abradale Press/Harry Abrams, 1979. 1993 edition published by Harry Abrams (Times Mirror).
Cousteau, Jacques. *The Ocean World of Jacques Cousteau: Guide to the Sea and Index*. New York: Danbury Press, 1974.
Cousteau, Jacques. *The Ocean World of Jacques Cousteau: Provinces of the Sea*. New York: World Publishing (Times Mirror), 1973.
Cousteau, Jacques, and Philippe Diole. *Three Adventures: Galapagos, Titicaca, The Blue Holes*. N. Y.: Doubleday, 1973.

Cousteau, Jacques, and Philippe Diole. *The Whale: Mighty Monarch of the Sea.* New York: Doubleday, 1972.

Cousteau, Jacques, with the Cousteau Society staff. *The Cousteau Almanac.* New York: Doubleday, 1981.

Cousteau, Jacques, with James Dugan. *The Living Sea.* New York: Harper and Row, 1963.

Cousteau, Jacques, with Frédéric Dumas. *The Silent World.* Oxford: Clio Press, 1989. Original copyright: Great Britain: Hamish Hamilton Ltd., 1953.

Cousteau, Jacques, with Mose Richards. *Cousteau's Papua New Guinea Journey.* New York: Harry Abrams, 1989.

Cousteau, Jacques, with Alexis Sivirine. *Jacques Cousteau's Calypso.* New York: Harry Abrams, 1983.

Films by Jacques Cousteau

In addition to early documentaries, Jacques Cousteau produced more than seventy films for television through his several television series and three full-length feature films: *The Silent World, World without Sun,* and *Voyage to the Edge of the World.* A list of Cousteau films available on videocassette is included in the Cousteau Society website: <www.cousteausociety.org/filmsC.html>.

Related Books and Websites

Cousteau, Jean-Michel, and Mose Richards. *Cousteau's Great White Shark.* New York: Harry Abrams, 1992.

Cousteau, Jean-Michel, with Mose Richards. *Cousteau's Australia Journey.* New York: Harry Abrams, 1993.

<www.cousteau.org>. The Cousteau Society website contains many articles, includes lists of Cousteau's many books and films, and provides links to related sites.

<www.dolphinlog.org>. The Cousteau Society's magazine *Dolphin Log* can be found online here.

<www.incwell.com/Biographies/Cousteau.html>. Sahlman, Rachel. "Jacques Cousteau."

INDEX

OTHER TITLES FROM LERNER AND A&E®:

ABOUT THE AUTHOR

Lesley A. DuTemple is an award-winning writer who lives in Salt Lake City, Utah. She has written five other books for young readers published by the Lerner Publishing Group: *Whales, Tigers, Moose,* and *Polar Bears* in Lerner's Early Bird Nature Book series and *North American Cranes* in its Nature Watch series. A licensed scuba diver, she has worked with the Cousteau Society for nearly a decade, contributing to *Dolphin Log,* the society's magazine for children, and *Calypso Log,* its publication for adults.

PHOTO ACKNOWLEDGMENTS

The Everett Collection, pp. 2, 58, 68, 73, 74, 77, 85, 95; Liaison Agency: (© Roger Viollet) pp. 6, 23, 53, (© Hulton Getty) pp. 20, 34, 38, 41, 71, (© Luongo) p. 91; Globe Photos, Inc.: (© Imapress/D.R.) pp. 10, 15, 25, (© Stephane Benito/Imapress) p. 99; UPI/Corbis-Bettman, pp. 28, 62, 86; Brown Brothers, pp. 35, 80; National Geographic Image Collection: (© Luis Marden) p. 46, (© Bates Littlehales) p. 78; Photofest, pp. 65, 87, 101; Archive Photos: (Archive France) p. 92, (Reuters/Regis Duvigneau) p. 104.

Cover photos
© Adam Scull/Globe Photos, Inc., front cover; Photofest, back cover.

Map by Laura Westlund, p. 19.